THE WORLD OF SKATEBOARDING

ADVANCED SKATEBOARDING: FROM KICK TURNS TO CATCHING AIR

Aaron Rosenberg

the rosen publishing group's
rosen central

Published in 2003 by The Rosen Publishing Group, Inc.
29 East 21st Street, New York, NY 10010

Library of Congress Cataloging-in-Publication Data

Rosenberg, Aaron.
Advanced skateboarding : from kick turns to catching air / by
Aaron Rosenberg.— 1st ed.
    p. cm. — (The world of skateboarding)
Includes bibliographical references and index.
Contents: The skate setting—About tricks—Low advanced tricks—
Medium advanced tricks—High advanced tricks.
ISBN 0-8239-3649-X (lib. bdg.)
1. Skateboarding—Juvenile literature. [1. Skateboarding.] I. Title.
II. Series.
GV859.8 .R65 2003
796.22—dc21

                                                        2002003958

Manufactured in the United States of America

CONTENTS

Welcome, skateboarders! Perhaps you read our book *A Beginner's Guide to Very Cool Skateboarding Tricks*, and now that you've mastered its contents and advice you want to expand your skills. Or perhaps you are already a skateboarder, and you want to jump directly into learning the more advanced techniques. Either way, this is the book for you. We'll talk about more advanced skateboarding tricks and give you a host of other useful tidbits besides—all about how to improve your skateboarding and to get the most out of the hobby itself. So read on!

You've already learned a bit about skateboarding, including the parts of the skateboard, the basic safety tips, and some basic tricks. But now you want to take it further. That's great—but where do you take it? Knowing where to skate is nearly as important as knowing how to skate. Should you skate on the street, in parking lots, or in skateparks? Different settings fit different styles of skating and different types of skaters. Which is best for you?

Ramps

If you haven't dealt with ramps yet, you probably will—most skateboarders do. That doesn't mean you have to use ramps, but you should at least know what they are and how they work, and try them to see if that type of skateboarding is for you.

You've seen ramps, of course, but what are they, exactly? Half-pipes, bowls, quarterpipes, and hips all help skateboarders to catch air. Most ramps are made from plywood, although some people use Masonite on the surface of the ramp, which is very smooth but can get too slick if wet and tends to get dusty. Ramps are concave, or arced inward. They can vary in size and shape, although a good ramp is at least twelve feet wide, and can be anywhere from one to fourteen feet high. So why are they curved? The curve of a ramp launches you high in the air, where you can do a number of different tricks. The higher you go, the more complex tricks you can do.

Miniramp and Vert Ramp

Miniramps and vert ramps are both halfpipes. They have two opposing walls to help skaters launch air tricks by going back and forth from one wall to its opposite. Miniramps are smaller versions of the vert ramp. They can range from about two to eight feet high. The most popular height is between six and eight feet. The miniramp is designed to do more technical tricks (i.e., a lot of flips and turns) whereas the vert ramp is designed to help you catch air.

The other type of halfpipe is the vert ramp. This is a specially built halfpipe that curves upward into a vertical incline. It is called a vert ramp after the word "vertical." A vert ramp is at least nine feet tall, and the steepest section of the ramp, near the lip, is vertical (straight up and down). The vertical part of the ramp launches skaters high into the air to do any number of tricks. Vert ramps used in competition are at least eleven feet tall—nine and a half feet of transition and a foot and a half of vert. Transitions are any part of the ramp that are

Vert ramps used in skateboarding competitions are large halfpipes that are at least nine feet tall.

curved. Skaters need at least sixteen inches of vert to get their boards completely vertical while still on the surface of the ramp. This sends skaters straight up and allows them to come straight down and against the vert wall to gain speed that will send them up the opposite ramp. Get it? Speed and vert are the name of the game!

Other Ramps

The bowl ramp, or bowl, is as its name suggests, a ramp with concave transitions all the way around, like a giant mixing bowl.

A bowl ramp is not unlike the empty swimming pools that skaters first started riding in.

A quarterpipe is a ramp with only one concave transition. It is one-half of a halfpipe or miniramp, hence the name quarterpipe, and can be anywhere from one foot high to fourteen feet high. Quarters are good for small practice areas such as a driveway or parking lot. If you put two quarters together facing each other, you'll have a halfpipe with the ground being the flat transition area.

A hip ramp is made up of two launch ramps or quarterpipes, at an angle from one another and touching at one corner. The angle is called the hip because it juts out like a hip. A variety of creative tricks can be done using a hip ramp.

Some ramps also have escalators—that's where part of the lip, or coping (the top edge of the ramp), is not horizontal but slopes from one height to another

Different skateparks (and backyards!) have different ramps. Most use these basic types. You'll need to practice a lot to decide which ramps you prefer. It's best to work your way up—start with a miniramp, then a vert ramp. That way you've got time to get more comfortable on the board—and in the air.

Sponsorship

Most skateboarders dream of being sponsored—having a company pay you to skateboard professionally. What could be better for a skateboarder? You get a board with your name and design on it. You get to travel around the world, you get to skate full-time, and somebody pays for it. Sponsorship is hard to get, though. There are hundreds of professional skateboarders right now, and even more amateurs, all competing for sponsorship. So how can you get it?

The first thing you need to do is to become a very good skater. Then you have to show it off by winning competitions. This will make you known. Sponsors will have heard about you. Of course, there is a bit of luck involved. A lot of luck comes from timing. Skaters sometimes move from one company to another, leaving a spot open on their team. And if you're really lucky, and really good, some day one of those companies may offer to sponsor you. Then all that extra work will have been worth it.

Street Skating Vs. Park Skating

So which will it be, street or park? Let's consider the differences.

Street skating is more spontaneous and more immediate. Often you never know what obstacles you'll find riding on the street, so you take them as they come. Park skating, in contrast, has all the ramps, rails, and stairs set up. You know exactly what ramps you'll find there, and all of them are specifically made for skaters. In street skating, you're improvising, using existing objects as ramps and rails. These include handrails, concrete benches, lawn boarders, and different kinds of stairs. Street obstacles are not built for skating, so they are more challenging—and more risky!

Street skating is also more open. You start as soon as you skate out the front door, and you don't stop until you get back home. The world is your skatepark! You can skate in one spot for hours or move from spot to spot as you see fit. There aren't any lines, and you don't have to buy tickets and wait your turn. In a skatepark, you have to pay to get in, then wait patiently for your turn at whatever ramp or rail you want to skate.

It sounds like street skating is the better option, doesn't it? But let's look at the other side.

Skateparks maintain their equipment. You know the ramps and rails are in good repair.and are not going to break on you—or under you. When you're street skating, no one's checking to see if that box is sturdy or rotten, and whether there are rusty nails in it or not.

Skateparks have people to supervise the skaters. That does mean you're being watched, but it means everyone else is, too. If someone cuts you off on a ramp, they'll get pulled aside. If you get hurt, there's someone there to take care of it right away. If you're street skating and get hurt, you may have to limp back home yourself before you can get any medical attention.

Skateparks are built specifically for skateboarders. You're welcome there, which means no one will hassle you. You're there to

When you street skate, the whole world becomes a skatepark, and the possibilities are endless.

skate, and so is everyone else. When you're street skating, you may get yelled at—even chased away—because you're in people's way.

Skateparks also give you a place to meet other skateboarders. You can exchange stories, trade tips, learn new tricks, and generally make friends. When you street skate, you might find other skaters, but you might not.

So does that mean skateparks are better?

The real answer is that both are good, but for different reasons. You have to decide what you're interested in. Do you want more

Skateparks have staffs that are there to help the skaters, to maintain the equipment, and to ensure safety.

risk but more freedom, or do you want more structure and stability? Are you looking to make friends or to spend time by yourself? There's also the question of availability. If there isn't a skatepark near you, you have to be content with street skating. Ultimately, whichever way works for you is fine, as long as you're happy skateboarding.

Most things in life can be organized into categories, and skateboarding tricks are no exception. Why should you care about categories? Breaking down the types of tricks is important when you begin to learn them.

Trick Types

Let's say you're practicing a 50-50 grind, and then you want to move on and try a 5-0 grind. They're both grinds, so you know they have some features in common. That makes it easier for you to learn the second one because you already have an understanding of the basic principles. Otherwise, you'd have to learn how to do a grind all over again before you could work on the 5-0.

It also helps to know your own strengths and weaknesses. Some people are really good at grabs. Others are better at stalls. Which are you? If you know you're good at grabs, you can concentrate on those more

Injuries

Skaters get hurt, just like all athletes in demanding sports. Let's face it—skateboarders twist and turn and leap and land, all on a small piece of wood with small wheels under it. Skaters are bound to get hurt sometimes.

The most common injury for skateboarders is a sprain: ankles, knees, wrists, elbows, shoulders—any of the body's joints. Doctors often recommend the R.I.C.E. method for treating sprains.

R–Rest   Stay off your feet whenever possible, and try not to use the sprained joint.

I–Ice   Icing the joint during the first twenty-four hours after the injury does two things—it numbs the injury, which helps reduce pain, and it controls swelling, which helps the healing process.

C–Compression   Wrap the joint with some sort of dressing or bandage, but not too tightly. You need to let the joint breathe, but you want to hold it still.

E–Elevate   When sitting or lying down, try to keep the joint higher than your chest to keep it above your heart. This keeps the blood from rushing to the joint, which helps to reduce the swelling and the pain.

to show off your skills. If you know you're weak on stalls, however, you can look for more advice on those tricks and can get in more practice time to improve yourself.

It also helps to talk to others. If you're comparing notes with another skater, you don't want to say, "I can do this one trick where I jump up in the air and bring the skateboard with me." You want to say, "I know the ollie already." That way you both know what you're talking about. The same is true with types of tricks. If you can say, "Hey, are you any good at airs? I've been having a hard time learning those," you both know what you're talking about, and you're more likely to get useful advice, tips, and even shared stories. That doesn't mean you have to shove each trick into a neat little box and label it, but it helps to discuss what you're doing and to have a name everyone else will recognize.

Here are the basic trick types and styles:

Flatland

These are tricks that don't use any inclines—you skate on the ground or some other flat surface. Flatland skating and street skating are terms that are used interchangeably. That doesn't mean your board stays flat on the ground, but you don't need ramps or anything else besides the ground and possibly obstacles.

Grabs

These tricks involve using one of your hands to grab somewhere on your deck while you are in the air. They can be done on both the street and ramps.

A railslide is a common trick where you catch air and move the bottom of your board along a handrail.

Grinds/Slides

These tricks involve moving the bottom of your board or the trucks along the edge or the top of an object.

Stalls

These tricks are done on curbs, railings, or ramps. They involve getting your board into a sliding or grinding position without actually doing a slide or grind. In other words, they focus on balancing your board on something for a few seconds without moving forward and then pulling off the object.

Vert

This is a style of skating performed on vert ramps, specifically tricks that are performed while in the air.

There are other trick categories, and some people invent their own. It is important that you know what you're talking about and whether one trick relates to another, and that you can discuss tricks with other skateboarders.

You already know how to ollie and nollie, to kickflip and pop shove-it. Each is a good trick, but they are the basics. Knowing them means you are ready to learn more advanced tricks.

The tricks in this book are divided into three categories: low, medium, and high. That's not the amount of height you need for each trick, it's how difficult they are compared to each other. Low advanced tricks are the least difficult advanced tricks to learn. They're harder than the basic tricks, but not by much. Start with these and work your way up, making sure you've mastered each trick before you move on to the next one. Some of them require that you can do easier tricks as well.

Manual

A manual is a trick that lets you ride balancing on your back wheels only.

1 Push off and put your front foot in the middle of the board and your back foot on the tail.

Push down on the tail and bring the front wheels off the ground. Balance and hold this position. Try not to have your tail drag on the ground—you want the front wheels just off the ground, but that's it. **2**

3 When you slow down or lose your balance, put the front wheels on the ground and ride off.

You can also do a nose manual—that's when you ride on only your front wheels. To do a nose manual, you put your front foot on the nose of the board and your back foot in the middle of the board. Now just push down with your front foot until the back wheels are off the ground. Be careful not to push down too hard on the nose, or you could wind up flipping over!

50-50 Stall

Before you try a 50-50 stall, you need to be sure you can do ollies and 180 ollies.

1. Start out by approaching the curb or ledge straight on at a medium speed.

2. Before meeting the obstacle, ollie and turn 90 degrees. Now you are in the air waiting to land on the object.

3. Land with both trucks on the edge. Keep your weight centered and balanced on the board.

Now stall—this means you hang there. This isn't a grind, so you're not supposed to be moving along the object.

4

When you're ready to come out of the stall, hit your tail, ollie, and turn away from the object. Land and ride away.

5

Boardslide

When you're first learning the boardslide, find an obstacle no higher than your knees. You can work your way up to larger obstacles later, after you've mastered the basics. You'll need to know how to ollie to do this trick.

Approach your target at an angle and at medium speed. Don't go too slowly, or your board will fail to slide on the object.

1

When you're next to the obstacle, do a 90-degree ollie onto it so that the side of the board is facing forward. Keep your shoulders perpendicular to the obstacle. It helps to focus on the middle of your board as you slide so that you can keep balanced.

2

Boardslide (continued)

3 Land balanced on the obstacle. Your board should slide forward.

4 When you're ready to get off, just turn your body and feet the way you want to get off. If the obstacle has a corner or lip in the way, you may need to angle up to get clear. (Note: This is a difficult trick for some people. Don't give up.)

50-50 Grind

In order to grind, you need to know how to ollie. Pick a ledge with coping as your target. The corner of a curb works fine.

1 Approach at a good speed from a shallow angle—you'll need some momentum to grind. Make sure your front foot is near the two back bolts on the front truck.

2 Ollie high enough for both trucks to be on the ledge, then push the nose down so the front truck is on the ledge.

3 Now push forward to grind. You need to keep your balance slightly forward so that the board grinds along the edge.

When you start to slow down or you reach the end of the ledge, lean back a little, lift the front truck off, and turn away. The back truck will follow.

4

Boneless

1 Start out with your front foot just behind the front truck bolts. Now reach down with your front hand and grab the toe edge of the board in front of your back foot.

Take your front foot off the board and slam it onto the ground behind you (on the heel side). Use this to jump off the ground, keeping the board under you with your front hand.

2

In the air, turn 180 degrees and land a fakie (with the tail of your board going forward).

3

Kick Turn

This is a ramp trick, so you'll need a miniramp or a vert ramp.

1 First, ride up the transition until you reach just below the lip.

Now shift your weight to your back foot and let the front wheels lift off the surface. **2**

3 Push down on the board with your back foot and, at the same time, turn your chest to face the bottom of the ramp.

Now push down on the front again so that the wheels touch the ramp, and ride back down. **4**

Drop In

To do tricks in a halfpipe, you must first know how to drop in. A drop in gives you speed and sets you up for all halfpipe tricks. First, find a small halfpipe. A three- or four-foot halfpipe is good to learn on.

1 Place your tail on the coping so that your trucks and wheels hang over the edge. Put your back foot on the tail and your front foot right behind the front bolts. Keep your weight on your back foot.

2 Now lean forward and shift enough weight to your front foot for the front truck to lay on the ramp. Be careful to balance! If you don't put any weight back on the tail after you lean in, you'll simply flip over. You also don't want to put everything onto the tail as you go down, or you'll flip up instead, and the board will shoot out from under you.

3 Keep both trucks on the ramp as you ride down to the flat bottom.

Want to Be Famous? Invent a Trick!

Don't believe it? Here are a few examples:

In the eighties, Eric Dressen tilted his 5-0 grinds a bit toward bluntslides, dubbed this move the salad grind, and made history. (Salad. Dressen. Yes, it's bad.)

Sal Barbier thought Brian Lotti's last name sounded a bit like "lottery," so he dubbed one of Brian's tricks "the big spin," for a scratch ticket in California.

Neil Blender invented the frontside air backside grab (in back of the front foot), and dubbed it the lien air. "Lien" is "Neil" spelled backward. (According to Neil, though, you have to "lien" (lean) in to make it.)

Mike Smith was the first to pull off a particular grind—back truck on, front truck below coping. Now it's called the Smith grind.

Josh Kasper took the benihana to another level by including a stare down in midair. That's now called a Kasperhana.

Blasting out of a vert ramp, with arms and legs sticking out to form a "T," and pulling it was something that only Christian Hosoi could do. Now it's called a Christ air.

Alan Gelfand aired out of a pool, front side, without using his hands, changing skateboarding forever. Now it's called an ollie.

Steve Caballero was the first one to spin a fakie 360 air, without grabbing. Not surprisingly, it's called a Caballerial now.

Tony Hawk and Lester Kasai decided to come up with a new trick. They figured they needed a catchy name if the trick was going to be a hit, so they named it the Madonna after the singer. Apparently it worked.

OK, so you've learned all the low advanced tricks. Then it's time to move on to some harder ones!

Rock 'n' Roll

This is a ramp trick, so you should be comfortable dropping in.

1 Drop in and approach the opposite ramp.

On your way up to the coping, keep your back foot on the tail and your front foot on the first two bolts of the front truck. **2**

3 Push down on your tail so your nose lifts and your front trucks reach over the coping.

Rock 'n' Roll (continued)

Then stall the board on the lip in a boardslide position, but not moving.

After a few seconds, place your weight on the tail so that the front trucks lift back over the lip.

Lift the nose high enough to clear the lip and rotate the board 180 degrees. Make sure your front truck doesn't get caught on the coping.

Push down slightly with your front foot, so your front truck is back on the ramp, and roll down the ramp.

Air

This is a vert trick. You can catch some air flying off a homemade ramp or even riding off a ledge. For this trick, however, you use a vert ramp to launch straight up in the air and come down on the ramp. Learn to catch vert air so you can do more difficult vert tricks.

1 Ride up the transition. As you rise above the lip in the air, reach to grab the board. You can grab the board any way you wish. You need to grab the board to have it stay beneath your feet.

2 Start to turn. It is easier to turn backside (with you chest facing the flat bottom) when first learning this trick.

3 Once you've finished turning, and your nose is facing toward the flat bottom, let go of the board as it passes below the coping and push hard against the ramp as soon as possible. Once all four wheels are planted on the surface of the ramp, slowly straighten out your legs as you ride down the transition.

Heelflip

The heelflip is basically the same trick as the kickflip, except that you flip the board in the opposite direction by using your heel.

1 Put your feet in the ollie position, but with your toes hanging over the edge of the front of the board.

2 Now ollie. Once your board levels out in midair, push down on the toe side of the board so that it flips.

3 After one complete flip, land on the board and ride away.

Indy Grab

This is a fairly simple grab, so it's a good way to start learning this type of trick.

1 Move forward slowly on a flat surface. Now ollie as high as you can, bending your knees as much as possible since you have to be able to reach the board with your hand.

2 At the top of your ollie, grab the toe side of your board with your right hand (left hand if you're goofy). Hold the grab until you're about to touch the ground.

3 Let go of the board, bend your knees to absorb the shock, land, straighten up, and ride away.

Mute Grab

A mute grab is when you grab the toe side of the board with your left hand (right hand if you skate goofy footed).

1 Ollie and grab your board while you're in the air. If you're ollieing off a ramp or some other obstacle, you should grab your board and hold it. If you're just skating flatland and ollie off the ground, you should just grab the board briefly and let go.

Mute Grab (continued)

2 As you come down, release the board before you land.

Tail Grab

This grab is less difficult because it's easier to reach the tail.

1 Ollie as high as you can.

Crouch down and grab the tail with your right hand (left hand if you skate goofy). **2**

3 Let go of the tail and land over the trucks. It's important that you let go of the tail quickly or you'll have trouble landing.

Half-Cab

Before you try a half-cab, you should be comfortable with ollies and fakie ollies. Learn how to land the half-cab before doing it over obstacles.

1 Ride fakie on a flat surface and ollie.

Rotate 180 degrees.

2

3 Land with the nose going forward and roll away.

The term "half-cab" is derived from the Caballerial, invented by the famous skateboarder Steve Caballero. The Caballerial is a 360-degree turn from fakie usually done on vert ramps. Note the half-cab, or one-half of a Caballerial, is a 180-degree turn.

Now we get to the really advanced tricks! Be sure that you've learned the others first and that you're comfortable with them—advanced tricks often combine easier tricks.

Varial Flip

The varial flip is a combination of a kickflip and a 360-degree pop shove-it.

1 Put your front foot in the kickflip position (similar to an ollie, but with your front foot hanging off slightly, toward the edge of your board) and your back foot in the pop shove-it position.

2 Now kick with your back foot as if you were going to do a 360-degree pop shove-it.

3 As the board starts to rotate, flip the board with the toes of your front foot as you would for a kickflip. The board should be spinning like a pop shove-it and a kickflip at the same time.

For the complete trick, the board should spin 360 degrees and flip once, both at the same time. If done right, the board will be spinning so fast that it will be hard to judge when it is in the upright position to land. You must develop a feel for when the right time is to land. This trick is all about timing. Stay over the board and land it with your feet over the trucks.

4

Ollie Impossible

This one is tough to learn, so don't give up if you can't get it at first.

1 Roll along at a comfortable speed on a flat surface. Place your front foot right in front of the nose. Your back foot should be on the tip of the tail, and your toes should hang off the tip of it.

Now snap the board like an ollie.

2

3 Here's the tricky part! Don't move your front foot forward to even the board out. Instead, slide your front foot off the board.

35

Ollie Impossible (continued)

4 Now sweep your back foot under you to make the board flip around your back foot. The board will flip backward 360 degrees, touching your back foot the whole time.

After the board completes its rotation, bring your front foot over the nose to stop the board from turning over again.

5

6 Now land with the board under your feet. When you're first learning this trick, you might want to practice flipping the board around your back foot with your front foot on the pavement.

Handplant

This is another ramp trick.

1 Ride up the transition and grab the board with your front hand just below the lip. Reach out with your back hand, and plant it on the lip.

Ride up beyond the ramp and grab the lip so your arm pushes your body straight up into the air. Your position is now basically a one-handed handstand, while holding your board with your free hand.

Now pull your body toward your arm and let go of the lip.

Fall back to the ramp, and ride back down.

Wallride

To do this trick, you need to be able to ollie at least two feet off the ground.

Ride toward a wall at a 45-degree angle. Get ready to ollie at the wall, and keep your eyes on the spot you want to wallride.

Wallride (continued)

Ollie up, but don't level out. Instead, bring your back foot up in line with your front foot while pushing the board toward the wall. Push your heels forward and your toes back. The board should be parallel to the ground.

2

 **3**

Now snap your toes forward, pushing the board up against the wall. You only want the balls of your feet on the board while you're wallriding, otherwise you won't be able to stay upright. If you do this right, you should be able to ride the wall for a second or two.

To get off a wallride, bend your legs a little (if they aren't already). **4**

5 Pop the tail and jump away from the wall.

Now level out the board with your hand by pulling your wrist in. Keep your feet flat against the deck.

Extend your legs a little to absorb the impact, land, and ride off.

Pros' Injuries

The first time you get hurt, you'll probably say, "I guess I'm not cut out for this skateboarding stuff." Why not? Do you think that only amateurs get hurt?

The truth is, everyone gets hurt—skateboarding is risky, and you will fall down. Most falls happen while you're learning a new trick.

Josh Kasper says that injuries happen all the time, and the only thing you can do is rest up, use the downtime to plan ahead, and get back to the skateboard once you're healed. His worst injury happened down in Mexico—he wound up with three fractures, a chipped heel, a pulled hamstring, and a nerve injury.

(continued on p. 40)

[continued from p. 39]

Tony Hawk admits he gets scrapes, sprains, and bruises all the time, and says you just learn to live with it.

Steve Caballero says it comes in spurts for him. He won't get hurt for a while, and then suddenly he'll get hurt all the time. His worst injury was a broken ankle.

Mike Vallely says he gets hurt daily, and every few years he's injured severely and has to take time off to heal. His worst injury was a torn shoulder muscle.

Donny Barley's worst injury was a rolled ankle, complete with torn ligaments.

Charlie Thomas's worst injury involved three broken bones—all in one foot!

All the pros agree on some points. First off, when you're injured you need to rest. Don't go hopping back on the skateboard after a day or two—wait until the doctor says it's OK. If you go back too soon, you may not heal fully, and that injury could bother you for the rest of your life.

Also, keep busy while you're hurt. Read, watch videos, play on the computer, catch up with family and friends. Don't lose touch with skateboarding, either—keep track of what's going on, check out Web sites and read magazines, and generally keep informed. They also say that, yes, after being injured you may be nervous skateboarding again—especially on the trick that knocked you down. But you have to get back up there and start riding again. The more time you spend back on your board, the stronger your confidence will get, and the more comfortable you'll be again. Hey, if it works for the pros, it'll work for you!

GLOSSARY

bowl ramp A ramp with concave transitions all the way around, like a giant mixing bowl.

demo Skateboarding demonstrations hosted by skateparks and shops, where pros and amateurs demonstrate their skills.

flatland A trick that doesn't use any incline, so you skate on the ground or some other flat surface.

grab A trick that involves using either hand to grab somewhere on your deck while you are in the air. Grabs can be done on both street and ramps.

grind A trick that involves moving the trucks of your board along the edge or top of an object.

halfpipe A ramp with two opposing walls, so that it dips down in the middle and back up on either side.

hang up While trying to drop back in off the coping after completing a trick, the truck that was above the coping does not clear it on the way back into the transition; this often results in a slam, but it can be pulled off by some.

hip ramp Two launch ramps or quarterpipes, at an angle from one another and touching at one corner. The angle is called the hip because it juts out like a hip.

miniramp A small halfpipe.

park skating Skating in a skatepark, using ramps and surfaces specifically designed for skateboarding.

quarterpipe A ramp with only one concave transition.

ramp A curved or inclined surface built to let skateboarders perform tricks in midair.

roll-in A smooth convex transition going from a flat platform into a steep transition.

slide A trick that involves moving the bottom of your board along the edge or the top of an object.

stall A trick that involves balancing your board on something for a few seconds without moving forward and then pulling off the object.

street skating Skating without using any ramps or anything but found obstacles.

trick A particular maneuver you learn to do while skateboarding.

vert This is a style of skating performed on vert ramps, specifically tricks that are performed while in the air.

vert ramp A specially built halfpipe that curves upward into a vertical incline.

FOR MORE INFORMATION

Organizations

Skatepark Association of the United States of America (SPAUSA)
2118 Wilshire Boulevard #622
Santa Monica, CA 90403
Web site: http://www.spausa.org/associations.html

Skatepark.org.
Mark Stosberg
914 East Main Street
Richmond, IN 47374
Web site: http://www.skatepark.org

United Skateboarding Association
P.O. Box 986
New Brunswick, NJ 08903
(732) 432-5400 ext. 2168 or ext. 2169
Web site: http://www.unitedskate.com

Web Sites

Due to the changing nature of Internet links, the Rosen Publishing Group, Inc., has developed an online list of Web sites related to the subject of this book. This site is updated regularly. Please use this link to access the list:

http://www.rosenlinks.com/wsk/adsk

FOR FURTHER READING

Caitlin, Stephen. *Skateboard Fun*.
Mahwah, NJ: Troll Communications, 1988.

Choyce, Lesley. *Skateboard Shakedown*. Halifax, Canada:
Formac, 1989.

Christopher, Matt, and Paul Mantell. *Skateboard Renegade*.
New York: Little, Brown and Company, 2000.

Davidson, Ben J. *The Skateboard Book*. New York: Grosset &
Dunlap, 1976.

Doeden, Matt. *Skateparks: Grab Your Skateboard*. Mankato, MN:
Capstone High-Interest Books, 2002.

Duncan, Frances. *Kap-Sun Ferris*. Toronto: Macmillan of
Canada, 1977.

Godfrey, Martyn. *Can You Teach Me to Pick My Nose?* New York:
Avon, 1990.

BIBLIOGRAPHY

"The Basics of Skateboarding." Retrieved December 2001 (http://www.geocities.com/skater4100/basics1.html).

Dj.Free. "Skateboarding-History and Styles." Retrieved December 2001 (http://www.referaty.sk/?referat=860).

Dunham, Dan, with Matthew B. Gross, Tim Leighton-Boyce, John Nixon, and Rick Valenzuela. "Skateboarding FAQ." October 1995. Retrieved December 2001 (http://web.cps.msu.edu/~dunhamda/dw/faq.html).

Qiao, Waley, and Jonathan Lee. "Sk8ter Fooyie." Retrieved December 2001 (http://members.tripod.com/little_zil8288/id19.htm).

Simplesam7's Skate page. Retrieved December 2001 (http://www.geocities.com/simplesam7).

Skateboard.com. Retrieved December 2001 (http://www.skateboard.com).

"The Skateboarding Basics." Retrieved December 2001 (http://www.geocities.com/jamen333/basics.html).

Smith and Feeble Skateboarding. Retrieved December 2001 (http://www.smithandfeeble.com/tricktips).

Ultimate Skateboarding.com. Retrieved December 2001 (http://www.geocities.com/pipeline/halfpipe/2950/tricks.html).

Watt, Andy. "Ramp Building FAQ." Retrieved December 2001 (http://www.cse.msu.edu/~dunhamda/dw/ramp_faq.html).

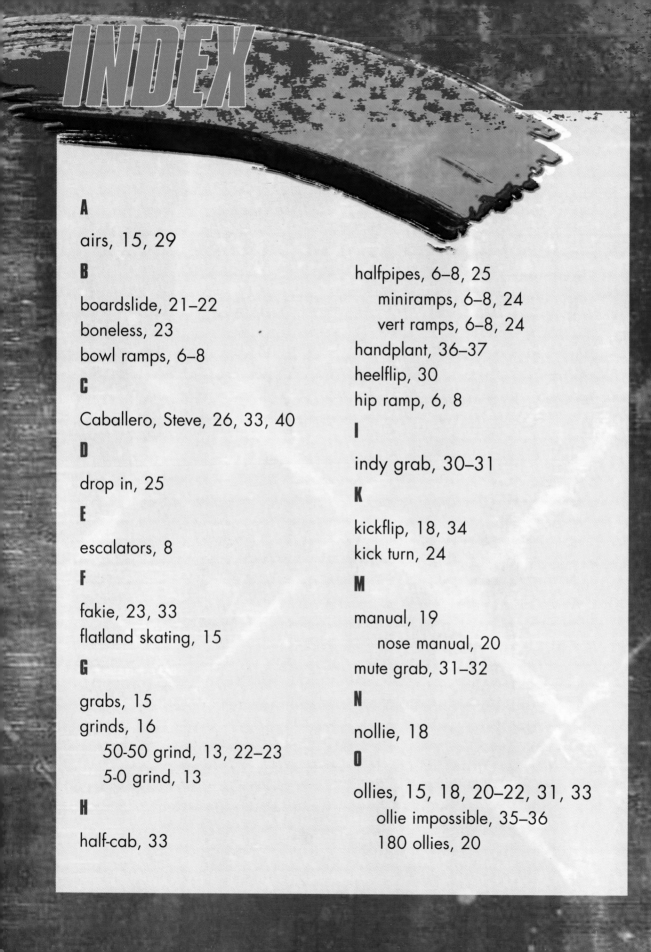

INDEX

CREDITS

About the Author

Aaron Rosenberg was born in New Jersey, grew up in New Orleans, and now lives in New York. He has taught college English, worked in corporate graphics, and now runs his own role-playing game publishing company (www.clockworksgames.com). He has written short stories, essays, poems, articles, novels, and role-playing games.

Acknowledgments

The editors would like to thank Sean McGuire at the Northridge Skatepark in Northridge, California, and Vic Vasquez from Val Surf in North Hollywood, California, for their time and cooperation.

Photo Credits

Cover © Stanley Chou/Getty Images; p. 4 © Nick Latham/Getty Images, Inc.; pp. 5, 8, 11, 12, 13 © AP/Wide World Photo; p. 7 © Bob Falcetti/Icon SMI; pp. 16, 18, 19–25, 27–39 © Tony Donaldson/Icon SMI.

Design and Layout

Thomas Forget

Editors

Mark Beyer and Nicholas Croce